# DAZZLING!

## Jewelry of
## the Ancient World

# DAZZLING!

## Jewelry of the Ancient World

Prepared by Geography Department

Runestone Press ◊ Minneapolis

# RUNESTONE PRESS • Rᚱᛐᚼᛏᛪᛏ

**rune** (r̄oon) *n* **1 a :** one of the earliest written alphabets used in northern Europe, dating back to A.D. 200; **b :** an alphabet character believed to have magic powers; **c :** a charm; **d :** an Old Norse or Finnish poem. **2 :** a poem or incantation of mysterious significance, often carved in stone.

Title page photo: A jeweler in Yemen crafts a piece from silver, a popular material in the Middle Eastern nation. As he works, the jeweler chews qat leaves, which contain a mild stimulant.

3 3113 01463 2444

Copyright © 1995 by Runestone Press,
a division of Lerner Publications Company

*Dazzling! Jewelry of the Ancient World* is a fully revised and updated edition of *Jewelry of the Ancient World,* a title previously published by Lerner Publications Company. The text is completely reset in 12/15 Albertus, and new photographs and captions have been added.

Thanks to Dr. Guy Gibbon, Department of Anthropology, University of Minnesota, for his help in preparing this book.

Words in **bold** type are listed in a glossary that starts on page 61.

Library of Congress Cataloging–in–Publication Data
   Dazzling! : jewelry of the ancient world / prepared by Geography Department, Runestone Press.
       p. cm—(Buried Worlds)
   Includes index.
   ISBN 0–8225–3203–4 (lib. bdg.)
   1. Jewelry, Ancient—Juvenile literature. [1. Jewelry, Ancient.] I. Runestone Press. Geography Dept. II. Series.
NK7307.D35 1995
739.27'093—dc20                                          94–21445
                                                              CIP
                                                               AC

Manufactured in the United States of America
1   2   3   4   5   6   – I/JR –   00   99   98   97   96   95

# CONTENTS

# THE ARCHAEOLOGIST'S TREASURE

For thousands of years, humans have worn jewelry, ranging from colorful shells to glimmering gold. The beauty of these ancient treasures dazzles modern collectors. But to **archaeologists** (scientists who dig up and study ancient objects), early jewelry gives clues about how ancient peoples lived and worked.

The careful study of jewelry can reveal a great deal about the religion, economics, art, technology, and social structure of an ancient civilization. For example, many people wore jewelry to honor certain gods or to display wealth and power. In some societies, advanced metalworking techniques enabled jewelers to make intricate pieces that represented the ideas and beliefs of a particular culture.

When archaeologists **excavate** (dig up) a piece of jewelry, they consider all other artifacts found alongside it. These remains, as well as historical literature, can help experts to determine how and why a person wore a particular piece.

## Ancient Sources

One of the biggest challenges archaeologists face in studying

*Archaeologists (scientists who dig up and study ancient objects) gently brush away dirt from jewelry found at an early Peruvian gravesite. Many ancient peoples buried decorative ornaments with the dead.*

*Mummies are bodies that have been preserved by a special chemical treatment. On top of the remains, mourners sometimes placed a portrait of the person who had died. This portrait, which shows the deceased wearing her favorite jewelry, helped archaeologists to understand how some adornments were worn in ancient times.*

ancient jewelry is figuring out how people wore certain pieces. Over time, jewelry can break or rot, depending on the material from which it is made. This deterioration can make it difficult to identify the function of a piece. For example, if the string on a pendant necklace has rotted away, experts may be unable to tell if the pendant was part of a necklace or a pin that lost its clasp.

This type of distinction can be made more easily when excavators find jewelry in graves. In many cultures, people adorned their dead before burial. For this reason, tombs sometimes hold the remains of bodies that are still wearing jewelry. From the position of a piece of jewelry, experts can distinguish a hair pin from a garment pin, an anklet from a bracelet, or an earring from a finger ring.

Archaeologists also use artworks, such as paintings and sculptures, to identify how ancient jewelry was worn. On tombs, palace walls, and pottery, early artists often represented the everyday life of their culture—including the wearing of jewelry. These depictions can illustrate fashions that may not be revealed by the piece of jewelry itself.

In one early painting from the ancient Syrian city of Palmyra, for instance, an artist showed people wearing rings on the upper joints of their fingers. This discovery helped

*Prehistoric humans made the earliest jewelry out of bone and shell.*

archaeologists to explain the small size of the rings found in the city's ruins.

## Organic Jewelry Materials

Since the prehistoric period, humans have made jewelry from organic (living or once-living) substances, such as the feathers, hides, bones, and fur of hunted animals. Over time, ancient people discovered rarer organic materials—including amber, coral, pearls, shells, and ivory—that could be fashioned into beautiful jewelry.

Amber is hardened resin, a sticky, yellowish brown substance produced by certain pine trees millions

*Live coral polyps extend their tentacles to feed in Australia's Great Barrier Reef. After the polyps die, they add their skeletons to the millions of others that make up a coral reef. The reefs provided ancient artisans with materials for making jewelry.*

of years ago. The trees gradually became buried by dirt or submerged in water, and the resins slowly hardened into underground lumps of amber.

Ancient people mined amber and shaped it into shiny beads, pendants, and other pieces. Amber was especially popular with the ancient Greeks, Romans, and Egyptians—cultures that lived along the shores of the Mediterranean Sea. These three civilizations imported amber from the Baltic region of northern Europe, which holds the world's largest supply of the substance.

Materials from the sea—including coral, pearls, and shells—commonly appeared in ancient jewelry. Coral, which is usually red, pink, or white in color, consists of the skeletons of tiny sea animals. The coral used by ancient jewelers had many different shapes and textures. One type of red coral, for example, was shaped like a pipe and could be strung as a bead. Divers find coral mainly in warm waters, such as in the Mediterranean Sea and in the South Pacific Ocean.

Pearls form inside the shells of oysters and other mollusks. When ancient people opened mollusks to harvest the meat inside, they sometimes discovered white, lustrous (shiny) pearls. Because they need no cutting or polishing to reveal their beauty, pearls were popular with ancient jewelers. But like any organic material, pearls decay over time. Archaeologists often find empty jewelry **settings** (mountings) that once held pearls.

Varied in size and color, shells were among the most popular jewelry-making materials of ancient times. Sometimes jewelers cut shells and shaped them into beads. Other artists simply pierced and strung shells. Merchants and traders, who brought shells inland from coastal regions, spread shell jewelry to markets throughout the world.

## Gold and Silver

Precious metals—such as gold and silver—are soft, reflect light, and have a natural shine that polishing enhances. Mined from the ground, these bright substances have been favored by jewelers for thousands of years.

Gold was one of the first known metals. In Egypt and in Mesopotamia (modern Iraq), archaeologists have unearthed gold cups and jewelry dating to 3500 B.C. The fine crafting of these objects shows

*Jewelers cut holes in bones and teeth before stringing them onto necklaces and other pieces.*

*Shiny, easy to mold, and rare, gold was a favorite material for jewelry makers. This Egyptian wall painting shows a goldsmith weighing the precious metal on a scale.*

that people had been working with gold for a long time.

The softness of gold makes it an easy metal to shape and to mold. When heated, it can be rolled into fine wire or hammered into thin sheets. For gold to be made into a hard object that keeps its shape, however, it must be mixed with tougher metals, such as copper or silver. Metal mixtures are called **alloys.**

Silver, another metal commonly used in ancient times, has a soft, white sheen. Silver reflects almost all of the light that strikes it, making it the shiniest metal. Although silver is harder than gold, it is still soft enough to hammer into various shapes.

When silver comes into contact with the chemical sulfur, a gray or black film forms on the metal. Sulfur is present in the air, especially the polluted air of modern times. For this reason, archaeologists must often clean and restore ancient silver jewelry to return it to its original state.

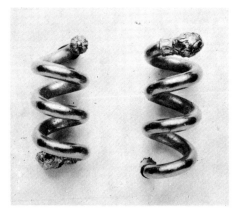

*Artisans from Cyprus, an island in the eastern Mediterranean Sea, shaped these hair or ear ornaments into tight spirals.*

*Craftspeople hammered and chiseled gold into realistic masks (right) or added gold wires and gold beads to earrings (below).*

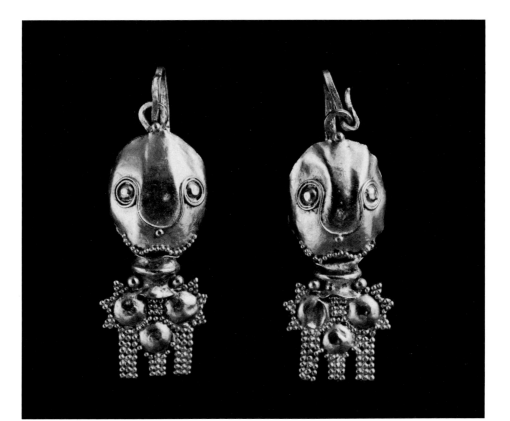

13

*This collection of Arab jewelry shows the variety of materials, including gold, silver, amber, and precious stones, that were available to artisans on the Arabian Peninsula.*

## Gemstones

Ancient jewelers often formed gold and silver into settings for gemstones, minerals that are shaped and polished to make jewelry. Many factors—including color, hardness, rarity, weight, and brilliance—determine a gemstone's value. Diamonds, emeralds, rubies, and other precious stones usually rate high in each of these categories. Semiprecious stones are generally softer and have more muted colors. Semiprecious stones include jade, agate, and lapis lazuli.

14

*To please well-to-do clients, jewelers mounted gemstones, such as lapis lazuli* (right) *and diamonds* (below), *into delicate metal settings.*

Most gemstones that ancient miners unearthed were irregularly shaped and had a rough surface. To shape and polish a gemstone, **lapidaries** (gem cutters) used a material that was as hard as or harder than the stone being cut. Archaeological evidence shows that early people made beads by striking soft stones with harder stones or by using tools like chisels and hammers. Ancient jewelers also used metal blades to cut, scratch, carve, and drill holes into soft stones.

*A gem cutter carefully presses a diamond—which is held tightly in a type of vice—onto a wheel sprinkled with diamond dust. The abrasive surface of the moving wheel slowly grinds away at the stone to create a facet.*

## THE CRAFT OF CUTTING

When miners dig gemstones out of the ground, the minerals usually have a rough surface. To make the stones into finished gems, skilled lapidaries (gem cutters) must cut and polish the material.

To determine how to shape a certain stone, experts consider the gem's hardness, its transparency, and something called its "index of refraction"—the angle that a ray of light bends as it goes through the material. Lapidaries then figure out which of the two main styles of cutting—faceting or cabochon—will show off a gemstone's best features.

In the faceting process, jewelers form many tiny polished sides that sparkle when light hits them. This type of cut is mostly used for very hard minerals, such as diamonds, rubies, or emeralds. Many different types of faceted styles

exist. The brilliant cut, for example, has 58 facets. Using the cabochon cut, lapidaries craft rounded, polished stones. Cabochons are usually shaped from softer minerals, such as turquoise, lapis lazuli, or agate.

Both hard and soft stones can be shaped only by materials that are as hard or harder than the gemstones themselves. For example, diamonds—the hardest gemstones—can be cut only with other diamonds. In this case, lapidaries usually grind diamonds into a dust and sprinkle the material onto a wheel, creating a surface similar to sandpaper. As the wheel rotates, the gem cutter presses the rough stone against the surface to grind away excess material. Although this method is slow and painstaking, if done carefully, it can produce beautiful and valuable results.

Early lapidaries eventually learned that the easiest way to shape gemstones was to grind away thin layers of material until the stone reached the desired form. At first, ancient jewelers rubbed stones against abrasive (very rough) surfaces, such as blocks of basalt or sandstone. Soon jewelers learned to make tools called laps, which consisted of a piece of wood, leather, or soft metal covered with a powdered abrasive.

After ancient people invented ways to make the laps turn, a lapidary could then hold a gemstone still while the abrasive surface moved. This technique gave

*Wealthy Romans supported a thriving jewelry industry throughout their far-flung empire. This hair ornament, made in North Africa in the third century A.D., holds inlaid emeralds in the center and pearls around the border. Twisted gold wires support hanging pearls and a sapphire.*

jewelers more control over the cutting of both hard and soft gemstones. Abrasives also aided lapidaries in polishing finished stones to a shine.

## Dating Jewelry

The value of jewelry is not only monetary but also sentimental. Since ancient times, families have passed pieces from generation to generation, sometimes carrying jewelry great distances. These circumstances can hinder archaeologists' attempts to date jewelry, especially when ancient pieces are found alongside more recent items.

The physical properties of jewelry also pose dating problems. Because the chemical makeup of gemstones and metals—two of the most common jewelry materials—change

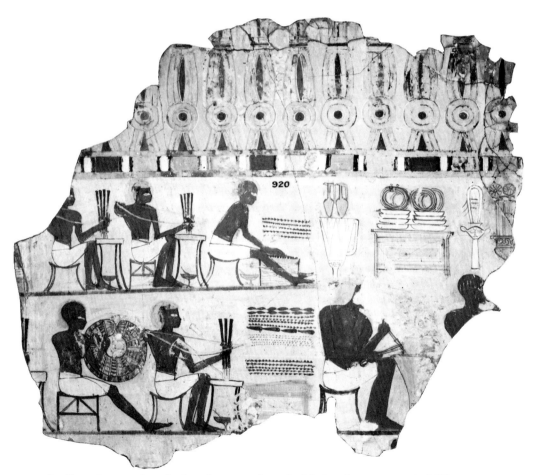

*An Egyptian tomb painting shows ancient lapidaries (gem cutters) drilling, stringing, and polishing beads made of carnelian, a hard, reddish precious stone.*

*Using advanced technology, archaeologists have photographed the granulation on an Etruscan earring at many times its actual size. Granulation involves the careful placement and joining of tiny gold grains to metal. By closely studying this example, experts can evaluate the metalworking skills of the Etruscans.*

little over time, there is no way to measure the age of most ancient jewelry. Some metals, such as copper, form films that can be dated by their thickness. For many other jewelry materials, however, dating is only guesswork.

Knowledge of the subject is the most valuable guide in dating ancient jewelry. Archaeologists study early texts and artworks to learn about the techniques and materials that ancient cultures employed in jewelry production. From this infor-

mation, scholars can sometimes determine the date and origin of a piece of jewelry.

Once experts understand ancient processes, they look at each piece of ancient jewelry under a high-power microscope. This close examination allows scientists to see in detail the metalworking and stonecutting techniques of ancient artisans. Archaeologists can then compare what they see with what they already know about ancient jewelry-making methods.

# ANCIENT JEWELRY OF THE MIDDLE EAST

The world's first civilizations arose in the Middle East more than 5,000 years ago. This region linked Africa and Asia and touched the eastern shore of the Mediterranean Sea, which offered Middle Eastern traders and travelers access to Europe. As they prospered, the inhabitants of the Middle East built cities and developed specialized industries, including jewelry making.

## Sumerian Graves

People in Mesopotamia, the land between the Tigris and Euphrates rivers, began building the world's first cities about 5,600 years ago. These rivers provided irrigation for crops and a transportation route for shipping wares to markets throughout the kingdom of Sumer and other regions.

Among the ruins of ancient Ur—a city in southern Mesopotamia—archaeologists have unearthed a vast amount of jewelry from graves. The most important finds came from royal tombs that date to about 2500 B.C. These sites held the bodies of kings and queens surrounded by their attendants, who were buried there to accompany

20

royal family members on the journey to the **afterlife.**

Specially dressed for burial, the Sumerian men and women in the royal tombs were heavily adorned with jewelry. Although strings and other materials that held the jewelry together had rotted away, archaeologists could identify many pieces by their positions on the bodies. On the remains of men, for example, excavators found headbands made of gold chain and beads. These items may have been used to keep headcloths in place.

The women in the royal tombs wore even more ornate jewelry, including intricate headdresses,

*Sumerian soldiers from Mesopotamia march into battle on this wooden panel found in a grave dating to 2500 B.C. Using shell, red limestone, and blue lapis lazuli, this inlay technique was commonly used to make Sumerian jewelry.*

*Gathered from several bodies in the royal tombs of Ur in Mesopotamia, this jewelry belonged to Sumerian nobility of about 2500 B.C. Sumerian women wore elaborate hair ornaments, heavy gold earrings, garment pins, and a variety of necklaces crafted from lapis lazuli, gold, and carnelian.*

crescent-shaped earrings, and tight-fitting necklaces called chokers. Decorative pins that once held clothing together were also common finds. In other Mesopotamian graves, experts have unearthed beads either strung into necklaces or sewed onto clothing.

The people of Mesopotamia tapped the resources of their surroundings for jewelry materials. Sumerian jewelers crafted most of their wares from gold, silver, blue lapis lazuli, and a red stone called carnelian, all of which were found nearby. Artisans also used obsidian—a black volcanic glass—as well as shells and baked clay.

Although the design of this jewelry was simple, the craftwork was very fine. Sumerian jewelers used the **inlay** technique to set stones within metal. Jewelers also created special looks with **filigree,** a method that consisted of twisting thin wires of gold and silver into complex patterns. They also alternated different colors of stone and

*Archaeologists unearthed these Sumerian headdress adornments from a grave at Ur. A round ornament inlaid with carnelian and lapis lazuli (above) is attached to strings of beads. Two gold disks (below) feature intricate filigree, a technique that involves twisting thin metal wires into patterns.*

metal to provide a balance of color and texture.

## Egyptian Jewelry

The Sumerians traded heavily with the Egyptians, who had settled farther west on the fertile land bordering the Nile River in northeastern Africa. By about 3100 B.C., the inhabitants of this area had established a wealthy and powerful civilization. The Egyptians soon expanded their realm, which by the 1400s B.C. stretched to other parts of the Middle East.

Wealthy kings called pharaohs ruled ancient Egypt. These leaders funded the construction of elaborate palaces and public buildings, as well as tombs hidden within enormous stone pyramids. The vast quantity of ancient ornaments excavated from the pyramids reveals the varied styles and techniques employed by ancient Egyptian jewelers.

The most common figures found on ancient Egyptian jewelry are animals, plants, and gods. Amulets, which people wore to ward off evil, took the form of cats, hippopotamuses, frogs, and snakes.

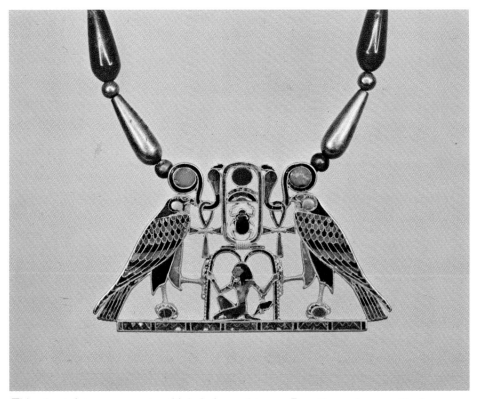

*This chestplate ornament, which belonged to an Egyptian princess, displays common ancient images of animals and gods.*

*Wearing elaborate headdresses and collars, the Egyptian pharaoh Tutankhamen and his queen decorate the back panel of a throne found in the ancient ruler's tomb. The artwork glimmers with gold, silver, and bright blue faience.*

Broad collars worn around the neck displayed date-palm leaves, poppy petals, bunches of grapes, and daisies. Jewelers often worked the images of gods and goddesses into designs on pectorals—large ornaments that covered the chest.

The Egyptians crafted their earliest jewelry from ivory and a variety of glazed stone beads. Jewelers ground up clay, glass, and minerals to make the glaze, which was melted and poured on the beads to give them a shiny surface. This technique allowed jewelers to imitate semiprecious stones with more common, less expensive materials. The **faience** style, for example, uses clay, a substance that is easily shaped and hardened into beads and other forms. When coated with brilliantly colored glazes, clay objects shine like polished stones.

The Egyptians employed many other techniques for making jewelry, including **ajouré, chasing, repoussé, granulation,** and **cloisonné.** These metalworking methods helped jewelers create beautiful pieces from gold, silver, and other metals. Using the ajouré method, jewelers cut intricate, open patterns out of metal sheets. The chasing technique involved indenting a pattern into a metal surface. Repoussé required a jeweler to hammer patterns on the back side of a metal sheet so that they stood out on the front.

Granulation, which was first used in Ur, was a painstaking technique that consisted of **soldering** (joining) tiny, round grains of metal to a metal background. Some ancient Egyptian jewelers so perfected this method of decoration that the soldering was not visible.

For inlay work, the Egyptians often used the cloisonné technique. Artisans made individual, empty cells—called cloisons—by soldering thin pieces of metal to a metal base. Many cloisons were combined to create a design or a picture. When this preliminary work was complete, the artisans filled the cloisons with different colors of ground-up enamel (a glassy material) and then baked the entire piece. After the enamel cooled, jewelers polished it to a shine.

These various materials and methods allowed the Egyptians to fashion a variety of ornaments. Necklaces ranged from a single string of round beads to broad collars of several strands called *wesekhs*. Some bracelets and anklets had rectangular glazed beads called *serekhs*. Diadems (crowns), belts, and other jewelry displayed stones inlaid in silver—which was rarer than gold in Egypt—and in electrum, a natural alloy of gold and silver. Earrings, which both Egyptian men and women wore, were either the pierced kind that went through the earlobe or a semicircular style that clutched the earlobe. *Shebyu* collars—strands of disk-shaped beads—and hollow, gold *awaw* bangles that fit on the upper arms were also popular among fashionable Egyptians.

## Tutankhamen's Treasure

The people of ancient Egypt had a religious faith that included a strong belief in the afterlife. To ensure their status and prosperity in the afterworld, the ancient pharaohs were buried in hidden tombs with great riches—including vast amounts of valuable jewelry.

Over the centuries, robbers broke into most of these tombs and stole the contents before archaeologists could study the remains. During the 1920s, however, archaeologists discovered the tomb of Tutankhamen, who ruled in the fourteenth century B.C. Although experts believe that Tutankhamen's tomb was one of the smallest and poorest in ancient Egypt, the original excavators were amazed by the enormous amount of gold and jewels contained within it.

One of the tomb's most important holdings was an ornate throne decorated with images of the pharaoh and his queen in gold, silver, and faience. Both figures wear elaborate diadems, broad collars, and silver bracelets. In addition, the pharaoh is dressed in a beaded girdle, which is tied around his waist like a belt. The excavators also found 13 bracelets decorating the arms of Tutankhamen.

Archaeologists compare Tutankhamen's tomb to a small museum. The vast contents give excavators the most complete record of the techniques of ancient Egyptian jewelers.

*Archaeologists discovered 13 bracelets on the arms of Tutankhamen. These pieces displayed many different styles, including filigree, granulation, and inlay.*

# ANCIENT JEWELRY OF ASIA

In Asia several ancient cultures thrived in what are now China, Southeast Asia, Korea, and Japan. Using available materials, these societies developed unique jewelry styles based on local religious beliefs and traditions.

## China

As early as 2000 B.C., civilizations emerged in north central China. Inhabitants built cities along the Huang (Yellow) River, which provided water to irrigate farmland and a convenient transportation route for trade between urban areas. The early Chinese civilizations set up strong hierarchical (class) societies, which is strongly reflected in how men and women wore jewelry. The amount of jewelry worn, for example, often signaled an individual's place in society. High-ranking members of a community showed great restraint in the amount of jewelry they wore. Many classes exchanged ornaments as symbols of friendship and trust.

Most ancient Chinese jewelry highlighted the ears, the hair, and the waist. Small ear ornaments dangled from silk threads, pretty ivory combs held hair in place, and ornate buckles decorated belts. Another important belt adornment was the *pei,* which hung from the belt on a pendant. Usually made from jade—a hard, green

*A painting from the tenth century A.D. depicts a Chinese woman adorned in a beautiful silk robe, as well as decorative hair ornaments, necklaces, and earrings. This traditional Chinese fashion originated in ancient times.*

stone highly valued by the Chinese—the parts of the pei made a soft sound as the wearer moved. In the presence of royalty, however, the shapes were kept silent to show respect.

Besides jade, which symbolized the highest social status, jewelers also made pieces from gold, silver, bronze, turquoise, and lapis lazuli. Organic substances, such as feathers, pearls, and coral, were also widely used. Artisans shaped these materials into images of people and animals, including tigers, tortoises, rabbits, birds, and fish.

*Gold and jade were two of the most common decorative materials used by ancient Chinese jewelers. Molded into the shapes of a ram's head and a pair of birds, two ornate gold beads* (above) *are edged with granulation. A jade pendant* (left) *features carved dragons.*

The hierarchical society of ancient China was also reflected in burial traditions. Jade was the most valued stone because the ancient Chinese believed it preserved the body forever. At first, the Chinese buried their dead with individual pieces of jade jewelry, such as bracelets, hairpins, and pendants. Eventually, however, craftspeople began producing large, intricately carved items that covered the face and chest. The wealthiest dead were completely encased in suits of jade joined together with gold, silver, or copper wire.

*Carved shapes dangle from a pendant on this ancient Chinese* pei, *an ornament used to decorate belts. Each piece of a* pei, *which was usually made of jade, carried intricate patterns.*

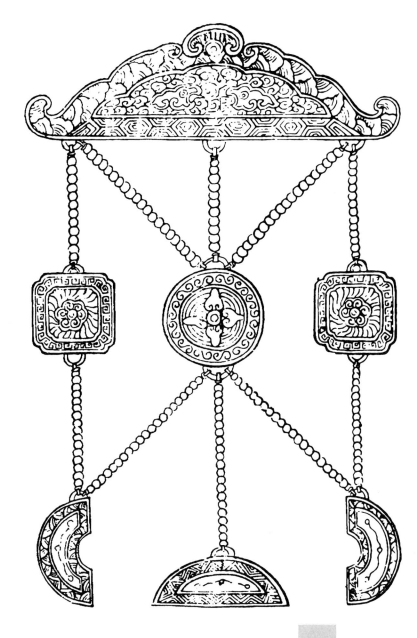

# THE JEWELS OF TAXILA

In the fourth century B.C., Taxila was a flourishing Asian city near the Indus River in what is now Pakistan. Highly skilled artisans in the city crafted beautiful jewelry, which merchants traded for other goods. In 326 B.C., Alexander the Great of Macedonia (an ancient region of Greece) conquered Taxila. Greek styles began to influence Taxila's jewelers, and as a result, archaeologists working in the ruins of Taxila have found pieces with Greek motifs.

Beads crafted from gold, carnelian, agate, shell, and lapis lazuli dominate the earliest jewelry finds at Taxila. These intricate beads came in many different shapes and sizes, with animal figures—a favorite Greek theme—being popular designs. As Taxila's artisans improved their skills, other common Greek motifs— such as the crescent shape and images of gods and goddesses— appeared in various forms. Pendants, earrings, and finger rings were often worked in filigree, granulation, and repoussé, all of which were techniques well-known among both European and Asian jewelers.

Although the Greeks influenced the design of Taxila's jewelry, the strict quality standards set by the city's jewelers always remained the same. Artisans expertly cut, engraved, and mounted stones and shaped gold into intricate ornaments. The discovery of these pieces revealed Taxila as one of the most important Asian sites for ancient jewelry.

*Archaeologists unearthed these gold ear plugs from the first century A.D. in Taxila, an ancient site in Pakistan.*

*Jewelers from Thailand crafted this thick, bronze bracelet as early as 800 B.C.*

## Southeast Asia

Southeast Asia includes 10 modern countries. Five of these nations—Myanmar, Cambodia, Laos, Thailand, and Vietnam—lie on a peninsula south of China. Malaysia also occupies a portion of this peninsula, as well as part of the large island of Borneo. Brunei takes up a small section of northern Borneo. The three remaining countries—Indonesia, the Philippines, and Singapore—are island nations. Since ancient times, the fertile soil and fish-filled waters of Southeast Asia have supported many thriving cultures.

The earliest jewelry of Southeast Asia dates to before 2000 B.C. and was made from shells and stones. Excavated from burial sites, this jewelry probably had religious meaning and suggests that early inhabitants believed in the afterlife. Over time, Southeast Asian jewelers learned to work with bronze.

Archaeologists have discovered many early bracelets shaped from this metal.

Gold was abundant throughout Southeast Asia in ancient times. By about A.D. 100, miners had learned to extract this precious metal on a large scale, and artisans had developed the skills necessary to work it into beautiful jewelry. From this time onward, gold became the most important material for jewelry making in the region.

Many ancient societies soon adapted gold to their religious and cultural traditions. In the Philippines, for example, burial customs came to include the placement of a thin, gold mask over the eyes, nose, and mouth of the deceased. When temples were dedicated in ancient Indonesia, ceremonial participants received gold finger rings whose weight was determined by the importance of the recipient. In Thailand, gold was buried in the foundations of temples.

Sculptures of royalty and other influential people reveal that the ancient Southeast Asians wore a wide array of gold jewelry. Heavy gold chains hang from the necks and a number of armbands crafted in repoussé stretch from the wrists to the shoulders. Rings decorate every finger, and ornate earrings dangle from pierced ears.

The vast supplies of gold in Southeast Asia attracted merchants from India, the Middle East, and Europe. These traders, who were always searching for new sources of the precious metal, eagerly exchanged their wares for locally made gold jewelry.

## Korea and Japan

Like the peoples of Southeast Asia, the inhabitants of ancient Korea are famous for their gold jewelry. Korea, which lies on a peninsula extending from eastern China, is now divided into the modern nations of North Korea and South Korea. Although little is known about the jewelry of Korea's earliest cultures, archaeologists have made some significant discoveries in the area dating to the first century B.C.

The most striking symbols of authority and power in ancient Korea were the gold crowns worn by the ruling class. To make a crown, an ancient jeweler cut a thin sheet of gold, bent it into a headband, and attached gold shapes that resembled tree branches or deer antlers. The surfaces of these crowns are often punched with patterns of dots. In addition, small pieces of jade and gold were attached to the crowns with gold wires. Less elaborate crowns consisted of headbands with floral patterns or geometric shapes cut into the metal.

In Japan, an island nation east of Korea, people wore very little

*Small circles hang from this ancient Korean crown, which was shaped from a thin sheet of gold.*

*The ancient Jōmon people of Japan crafted comma-shaped beads called* magatama *as early as 1000* B.C.

jewelry in ancient times. Early inhabitants made simple necklaces and bracelets from colorful shells and stones. Over time, Japanese jewelers learned to shape metal and to make glass beads. But most ancient Japanese adorned themselves with colorful silk robes and simple hair ornaments.

Both men and women wore combs to hold their hair in place. But experts believe that only Japanese women wore combs for decorative reasons. Archaeologists have discovered fragments of combs made by the Jōmon, a group that first settled Japan in about 10,000 B.C. Most early Japanese combs were crafted from wood or from bamboo, a tropical plant with a hollow stem. For added strength and beauty, the Japanese finished their combs with lacquer, a shiny varnish.

# PRIAM'S TREASURE

According to ancient Greek writings, Troy was a wealthy and powerful city ruled by King Priam. The Greek poet Homer made Troy famous in his stories of the Trojan War, a conflict between Troy and the Greek city of Sparta. Inspired by these tales, a German archaeologist named Heinrich Schliemann set out to find the remains of ancient Troy. In 1870 he began digging on the northwestern coast of Turkey, across the Aegean Sea from Greece.

During the excavation, Schliemann found that several cities had existed on the site. One of these cities had massive walls, well-built houses, and a hidden treasure of gold and silver—including enormous amounts of jewelry. Schliemann believed that the jewelry had been stored in the king's palace and named his discovery Priam's Treasure. Priam's Treasure consisted of beautiful crowns, earrings, bracelets, pendants, and almost 9,000 gold beads.

Many modern archaeologists disagree about which city in Schliemann's excavation was the Troy that matches Homer's writings. And many scholars doubt that the treasure of ancient jewelry belonged to King Priam. But the fine crafting and design of the pieces in Priam's Treasure have helped experts learn about the lives of the ancient Trojans.

*German archaeologist Heinrich Schliemann discovered a huge treasure of jewelry at the site of the ancient city of Troy in modern Turkey. His wife Sophie (right) models some of the elaborate pieces.*

# ANCIENT JEWELRY OF EUROPE

For Europeans of the ancient world, the Mediterranean Sea was truly "the center of the earth," as a translation of the sea's Latin name suggests. Merchants used this long, narrow body of water as their main transportation route. In fact, the history of ancient European jewelry is closely linked with navigation and commerce on the Mediterranean Sea.

## European Jewelry Techniques

Although they made and traded jewelry, the Phoenicians—who settled on the shores of the eastern Mediterranean—were famous as buyers and sellers of many other goods. These restless travelers and traders helped to spread jewelry-making techniques and jewelry styles to many parts of Europe, including what are now Greece and Italy.

In other parts of the Mediterranean, ancient civilizations, such as the Egyptians, had already developed strong jewelry traditions long before the Phoenicians engaged in commerce. Yet many of the same techniques and styles of jewelry are found throughout the region, where artists shared, translated, and updated methods to please the tastes of their wealthy clients.

Among the most popular techniques used for European gold pieces were filigree, granulation, and repoussé. Jewelry makers used these methods to craft a wide variety of ornaments, including earrings, bracelets, finger rings, torques (neck collars), fibulae (broochlike safety pins), pendants, armbands, diadems, and necklaces. Expressing popular styles of the time, jewelers turned out these goods to meet the preferences of their clients, most of whom were rich and socially prominent.

*Dating from the second century B.C., this necklace features intricate beadwork that ends in a crescent-shaped pendant. The crescent shape, an ancient symbol of a moon god, was probably imported to Greece from western Asia in the seventh century B.C.*

## Minoa and Mycenae

The country now known as Greece is made up of a mainland and many island groups. Crete, the largest and southernmost of the Greek islands, contains the remains of the ancient Minoan and Mycenean civilizations—both of which boasted strong jewelry-making traditions.

Large amounts of Minoan jewelry date from 1800 B.C. to 1400 B.C. Excavated pieces indicate that Mi-

*A drawing* (above) **shows Phoenician merchants offering their wares to buyers along the coast of the Mediterranean Sea. From their home in the eastern Mediterranean, the Phoenicians spread jewelry-making methods to Greece, Italy, and other parts of Europe. Gold ornaments, such as this pendant shaped like a wild goat** (left), **were popular among wealthy people on the Greek island of Crete.**

*A Minoan artist chose dogs and monkeys to adorn the middle of this earring, which has a hoop in the form of a double-headed snake. Disks and owl pendants hang from short chains that are further decorated with carnelian stones.*

noan artists had a flair for creating realistic scenes from nature. Archaeologists have found earrings in the shape of bulls' heads and pins expertly stamped with images of sea animals. Workers on Crete have unearthed hair ornaments, elaborate looped chains, and royal diadems of gold that show both a native Minoan style, as well as influence from the Middle East.

In about 1450 B.C., Crete was conquered by armies from Mycenae, a city on mainland Greece. The Mycenaeans adopted Minoan production methods and decorative techniques for making jewelry. These new settlers also had access to large deposits of gold. As a result, archaeologists working on Crete have uncovered Mycenaean jewelry that strongly resembles Minoan ornaments. Although they used filigree and granulation, Mycenaean goldsmiths excelled in repoussé work, especially beads with raised designs that were strung together as necklaces or bracelets.

The Minoan-Mycenean culture ended in about 1100 B.C., either

*Filigree, granulation, and inlay styles embellish this Etruscan ear stud from the sixth century B.C. A pin at the back allowed the wearer to fasten the stud into a small hole in the earlobe.*

from a military invasion or a natural disaster. Jewelry making declined in Greece for several centuries until commercial contact with Phoenician merchants and goldsmiths revived the jewelry craft.

## Etruscan and Greek Wares

By the eighth century B.C., Phoenician traders had expanded into the Greek islands, as well as into coastal areas of the European mainland. Some Phoenician merchants established outposts on the Italian Peninsula, where the Etruscan civilization was flourishing. The Etruscans traded their agricultural and mineral goods for luxuries imported from Greece. In time, the Etruscans began to produce and trade their own jewelry, improving on the techniques of Greek and Phoenician artists.

Etruscan jewelers probably had no rivals in their skill with granulation. Using the tiny gold beads, they fashioned complex scenes of nature, as well as simple decorative patterns. Sometimes the figures were in relief and the entire background

# CELTIC TORQUES AND FIBULAE

The Celts were an ancient people who lived throughout Europe beginning in about 700 B.C. This group, which divided itself into clans, inhabited lands as far west as the British Isles and as far east as Greece. Some Celts built towns, but most clan members settled in rural areas and farmed. The Celts also mined deposits of gold, silver, and bronze, and worked these metals into objects, such as tools and jewelry.

Celtic jewelers made a variety of pieces, including bracelets, anklets, and rings. Families often buried some of these valued items in the graves of their dead relatives. But excavation of Celtic burial sites shows that the most common jewelry pieces were fibulae (pins) and torques (collars).

The fibulae, which worked like modern safety pins, fastened heavy cloaks at the shoulder. Celtic artisans formed most fibulae into simple shapes and sometimes inlaid coral, stones, or glass into the metal. Celtic torques ranged from simple, undecorated rings to thick gold pieces adorned with patterns of interwoven curves and spirals. Women mainly wore these collars, but Celtic warriors sometimes put on torques for battle.

In modern times, the Celtic metalworking tradition is preserved in Ireland, Scotland, Wales, England, and Brittany (a region of France). Jewelers in these places still create intricate pieces that display their Celtic heritage.

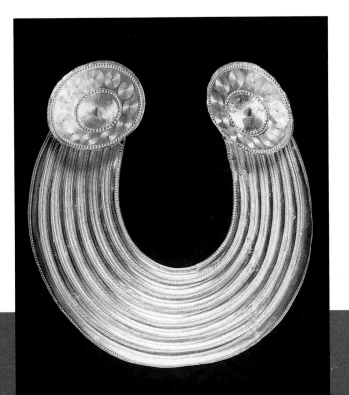

*Decorated with the repoussé technique, this gold torque (collar) was made by Celtic artisans in Ireland.*

was in granulation. Although filigree was initially unpopular in Etruscan lands, it eventually appeared on earrings, necklaces, and bracelets with great regularity. Wealthy Etruscan buyers were very fond of bright colors, and local goldsmiths introduced beads of porcelain or glass that were inlaid to brighten a gold metal design.

The Etruscan civilization began to wane in the fifth century B.C. At the same time, a revived Greek civilization introduced the Hellenistic Age. During this period, which lasted from the fourth century B.C. to the early first century B.C., Greek merchants traded in southern Europe, northern Africa, and western Asia.

During the Hellenistic Age, Greek artists experimented with Asian and European jewelry-making techniques. The Heracles knot (a type of square knot), the crescent shape, and colored stones became very popular among a new class of wealthy Greeks. Native Greek decorative styles included figures of Greek gods and goddesses. Skilled and creative, Greek goldsmiths soon produced a large quantity of fine gold and multicolored jewelry, which was traded throughout the ancient world.

A favorite design for Greek jewelers involved using small tassels or animal heads as hanging ornaments, especially on gold necklaces or gold earrings. The upper part of a pierced earring might have a small gold or colored disk to cover the hook for the earlobe. One or more pendants hung from the disk,

*Hanging ornaments were extremely popular among Greek buyers of the Hellenistic Age (fourth century to first century B.C.). This earring features rosettes at the top, followed by a mounting, twisted wires, and an hourglass-shaped figure that is decorated with granulation.*

*Greek jewelers used many artistic methods and images in their necklaces. This example from the fifth century B.C. features hanging buds strung between flowers.*

fashioned in the shape of goats, seahorses, birds, or even everyday items like wine jugs or bunches of grapes.

## The Roman Empire

Rome, a city on the Italian Peninsula, had been expanding its power in the Mediterranean region for several centuries. In 27 B.C., Augustus Caesar became the country's leader and set up the Roman Empire, which included most of Europe, as well as lands in Asia and Africa. Because the empire was so vast, archaeologists have uncovered Roman-era jewelry from as far north as the British Isles, as far west as

Spain, as far east as Syria, and as far south as Egypt.

At first, the Romans did not have their own styles of jewelry and borrowed liberally from Greek and Etruscan traditions. Bracelets were of varied designs, including a string of dangling gold spheres and a lifelike snake that twisted tightly around the wrist. Some bracelets were worn on the upper arms. Finger rings were popular for both well-to-do and ordinary Romans as signs of office, of betrothal, of wealth, or of social rank. From the Etruscans and other groups, the Romans adopted the use of fibulae to fasten their robes.

As the empire became richer and more powerful, fashions were

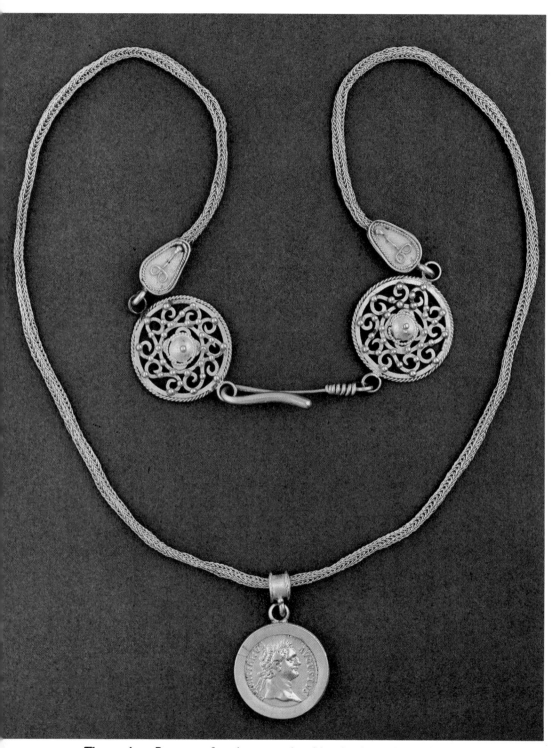

The ancient Romans often integrated gold coins into their jewelry. The pendant of this necklace is a coin that was minted in the first century A.D., during the reign of Emperor Domitian, who was known for his excessive use of personal adornments.

dictated from Rome. Citizens used their newfound wealth to buy ornate jewelry and Rome became a hub of jewelry making with its own workshops and jewelers' guilds (craft associations). Silversmiths and goldsmiths worked in the same quarter of the city. Other specialists included modelers, polishers, gilders, chiselers, and stonecutters. This congregation of craft laborers developed a distinctly Roman style of jewelry.

Typical of ancient Roman jewelry was the frequent—sometimes even haphazard—use of colored stones. Jewelers placed pearls, emeralds, sapphires, garnets, and many other showy gems in subtle gold settings. An innovation that was purely Roman was **opus interrasile,** in which artisans chiseled delicate lacelike patterns out of gold sheets. Sometimes they combined the chiseled work with coins and cameos (raised portraits). Later Roman jewelers also used inlaying and **niello,** a decorative method that set a black compound into an engraved metal space and then

*Worked in* **opus interrasile,** *a lacelike decorative technique, this bracelet dates to the late fourth century* A.D. *The Roman-era artisan who crafted the piece included an inscription that reads, "May you have fortune all your life."*

fused the compound with the metal.

## Northern European Styles

In the fourth century A.D., the Roman Empire began to break up and eventually split into western and eastern halves. To boost its defenses, the western empire used Germanic troops from northern Europe, and these groups—after being in contact with Rome—combined their own styles with those of the empire. Some Germanic groups took the opportunity to conquer former Roman provinces. The Anglo-Saxons, for example, invaded the British Isles in the fifth century A.D. Other Germanic peoples active in northern

*After the decline of the Roman Empire in the late fifth century A.D., jewelers in former Roman provinces, such as Britain, experienced shortages of raw materials. This seventh-century brooch from southern Britain features polished shells and colored glass—inexpensive goods compared to the gold, silver, and gemstones used while the empire was flourishing.*

Europe were from Scandinavia—what is now Denmark, Sweden, and Norway.

Northern European artists had long pursued their own designs. Torque and fibulae were favored jewelry-making techniques among Scandinavians. But sometimes goldsmiths adopted the styles of the peoples to the south, with whom they traded. Scandinavians, for instance, particularly favored the richly colored stones, especially garnets, that adorned Roman jewelry. Some jewelers mixed several techniques, combining a metal background with stamping, punching, and relief work.

The inhabitants of the British Isles had wholeheartedly adopted Roman styles. But after the empire's breakup, gold became scarce. As a result, Anglo-Saxon jewelers began using silver coupled with complex drawings outlined in niello. Nevertheless, gold was still reserved for important finger rings, as well as for use in gilding and inlay.

In both Anglo-Saxon and Scandinavian works, simple animal ornaments were popular, but there are also many examples of densely ornamented brooches for clothing. The famous Tara Brooch, for example, exhibits hammering, chasing, engraving, and gilding, as well as niello, granulation, and filigree.

Archaeologists and treasure hunters have unearthed most ancient European jewelry from graves or

*Noblewomen wearing necklaces, crowns, and other jewelry surround Charlemagne, who ruled much of Europe in the late eighth and early ninth centuries. Although the emperor allowed his rich subjects to display their wealth when they were alive, he made it illegal to bury fine jewelry in family tombs.*

from old stashes of goods that also include coins and other valuables. A sharp decline in finds of European jewelry can be linked to a decree by Charlemagne, a powerful emperor who ruled much of the European continent in the late eighth and early ninth centuries. His law prohibited corpses to be buried with jewelry—a practice he thought was both un-Christian and wasteful. As a result, archaeologists have found fewer and fewer ancient European ornaments dating from Charlemagne's time onward.

# ANCIENT JEWELRY OF THE AMERICAS

On the other side of the world, far from the early civilizations of the Middle East, Asia, and Europe, several ancient groups thrived in the Americas. The earliest civilizations of this region appeared in Mesoamerica, a narrow strip of land that joins North America to South America. Other civilizations arose along the mountainous western coast of South America and the plains and valleys of North America.

The various cultures of the Americas held much in common, including the skill of jewelry making. These highly religious groups crafted ornaments as a display of the wealth, status, and power of their rulers, who were often considered godlike figures.

## Mesoamerica

Ancient Mesoamerica—which includes the modern countries of Mexico, Guatemala, Belize, Honduras, and El Salvador—was the home of the ancient Olmec and Maya. The Olmec, the earliest of these two groups, thrived in the hot, wet lowlands of eastern Mexico beginning about 1200 B.C.

Excavations of Olmec tombs have revealed rich stores of jade jewelry, which was probably worn by early Olmec rulers to enhance their power and prestige. Jade, ranging in color from bright apple-green to deep blue-green, was prized for its cool, smooth texture. Olmec jewelers shaped jade into beads, pendants, and ear ornaments. Pendants often featured carved human heads or pairs of hands, while other pieces were delicately engraved with images of birds, reptiles, or jaguars. Some archaeologists believe that these animal images represented gods.

The Olmec religion—which included a reverence for the jaguar—strongly influenced the Maya, who settled in Mesoamerica as early as

*A stern face carved from jade stares from this ancient Olmec pendant found in Mexico. The human head was one of the most common themes in Olmec artworks.*

600 B.C. By about A.D. 250, the Mayan civilization was flourishing. Mayan workers built large cities that housed thousands of people, as well as ritual centers that featured majestic pyramids.

The artistic achievements of the Maya are evident in their jewelry, most of which was made of jade. In Mayan tombs, archaeologists discovered splendid jade beads of many shapes and sizes. Some were rounded, others resembled tubes, while still others were finely carved into forms of people or animals. The Maya probably buried these jade pieces with rulers and nobles as signs of wealth, power, and importance.

Mayan artisans also crafted ornate jewelry to adorn their leaders in life. These rulers put on the most decorative jewelry for ceremonies that honored the Mayan gods. Common pieces included pendants, bracelets, and anklets. Leaders also wore lip ornaments called **labrets** that were inserted

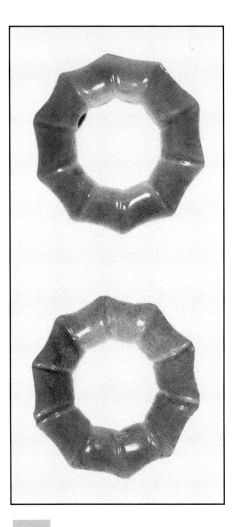

*Unearthed in Belize, this pair of Mayan jade ear flares was made to fit around the ear and stick outward. Jade was highly valued by the Maya and was often buried with the dead.*

through a hole cut in the lower lip. Carved pectorals featured scenes of human figures wearing elaborate jewelry, fine clothing, and feathered headdresses. Decorative nose pins were slipped through holes pierced in the nose. Although artists carved most of this jewelry from jade, they also made some items from shell or obsidian.

The Maya were expert stonecutters, but they never became skilled at working metal. The Aztecs, who controlled Mexico in about A.D. 1300—less than 500 years after the disappearance of the Maya— learned this technique and crafted gold objects of great beauty.

Aztec kings, who lived in splendor and ruled over enormous cities, wore fine jewelry that reflected their status. Aztec jewelers made royal adornments mainly from jade, turquoise, gold, and exotic feathers. Each of these materials held special meaning in the Aztec world. Stones of blue or green, for example, symbolized fertility and growth. Gold usually stood for fire.

Skilled Aztec goldsmiths employed many metalworking techniques, including gold beating and repoussé. The gold beating method consisted of pounding soft gold nuggets into thin sheets, which were then shaped into jewelry. Artisans also used gold sheets as backgrounds for mosaics—patterns or pictures made up of small pieces of stone, glass, or other material. The Aztecs are especially famous for their bright turquoise mosaics, which often decorated pendants, pectorals, and masks.

## South America

Some of the most important archaeological sites in South America were built by the Moche, a civilization that lived on the northwestern coast of Peru about 200 B.C. The Moche people built large ceremonial complexes that housed administrative and economic activities.

Artifacts of gold, silver, and copper excavated from these sites indicate that the inhabitants were skilled metalworkers. Jewelers flattened metal into sheets and soldered the pieces together to create beautiful combinations of gold, silver, and copper. Archaeologists believe that, to perfect such techniques, young Moche workers must have served as apprentices to older skilled technicians.

Moche rulers, whom the people revered as gods, commissioned elaborate ornaments from local metalworkers. The leaders wore this high-quality jewelry during religious ceremonies and were buried with it after they died. Archaeologists have been astounded by the delicacy of the jewelry in Moche graves. Some gold pieces, for example, contained many dangling parts, such as tiny disks, which may have been

*Early Aztec artists used the mosaic technique to decorate this two-headed serpent with small pieces of turquoise and shell. Experts believe that a powerful noble wore the large ornament as a pendant.*

designed to reflect sunlight as they moved.

Finely worked gold and silver beads crafted into figures of cats, peanuts, and spiders adorned Moche necklaces. Nose ornaments often displayed fancy animal designs, such as rows of golden seabirds, crayfish, iguanas, or other creatures. Artisans inlaid bright pieces of turquoise and shell into gold ear ornaments and strung tiny turquoise beads into bracelets that extended from the wrist to the elbow.

The Incas, another group skilled in metalwork, settled the coast of what is now Peru in the fourteenth century A.D. This civilization gradually extended along the Pacific shores of South America, including regions of present-day Colombia, Ecuador, Bolivia, and Argentina. By adopting some techniques of the Moche, the Incas developed a unique artistic style.

Headed by a godlike king, the Incan civilization was highly religious. Ruling families prayed to the sun god Inti and made governmental decisions at religious ceremonies. The leaders wore shiny gold jewelry to symbolize their association with Inti. Adorned from head

*Archaeologists removed jewelry, such as this small gold figure* (right), *from the grave of a Moche noble* (below). *The Moche, who lived along the coast of Peru, were highly skilled metalworkers who crafted gold and silver into intricate figures.*

to toe with gold necklaces, gold ear ornaments, and brightly colored clothing, Incan rulers provided a dazzling display for their people. Although gold was mainly reserved for leaders, it was also worn by distinguished nobles. The wives of these nobles wore elaborate gold ear ornaments.

The Incas, like the Moche, also used gold alloys to create works that ranged in color from copper-red to silver-white. Precious and semiprecious stones, including emeralds, lapis lazuli, and turquoise, as well as coral and pearls gave Incan jewelers a wide variety of colors to work with.

In 1532 Spanish conquerors destroyed the Incan capital of Cuzco and looted the empire for gold. Soldiers took all the gold artifacts they could find and sent the pieces to Spain to be melted into bars. For this reason, few examples of ancient Incan jewelry have survived, leaving archaeologists with only a sketchy record of Incan adornment.

## North America

By about 300 B.C., many Indian groups had settled in parts of what is now the United States. These peoples lived in villages, traded widely with other groups, and created their own artistic styles. The descendants of these early cultures developed more advanced skills in weaving, pottery, and jewelry making.

The Adena people inhabited the fertile areas of the Ohio and Mississippi river valleys in the eastern United States. They layered dirt to create enormous mounds in which they buried their dead. The Adena culture thrived for many centuries and eventually was replaced by the Hopewell culture by about 300 B.C. The Hopewell Indians constructed mounds as tall as 40 feet (12 meters) in giant geometric or animal shapes.

Inside these graves, the people placed a wide variety of jewelry crafted from pearls, stones, bones, copper, animal teeth, and shell. Not all of these materials, however, were readily available in the Hopewell region. Copper, for instance, originated in the northern Great Lakes area, while many shells came from the Atlantic Ocean. Archaeologists believe that the Hopewell Indians developed a vast trading network to obtain the materials needed for their jewelry and artworks.

Among the ancient jewelry in the Hopewell graves were pearls strung into necklaces and shells shaped into nose and ear ornaments. Jewelers also engraved gorgets—collars that covered the throat—with geometric designs or images of people or animals. Pectorals featured elaborate designs in repoussé. Experts believe that the Hopewell Indians placed this jewelry in graves as gifts for the deceased to use in the afterlife.

Personal ornamentation was very important to early North American Indian cultures. In addition to jewelry, which included headbands and headdresses, many Indian groups wore body paints for battle, public ceremonies, and religious rituals. This adornment often had spiritual meaning. Turquoise paint, for example, held special significance for a Cliff Dweller group called the Anasazi.

The Anasazi and other Southwest cultures sometimes built their homes and villages into the steep canyon walls of the southwestern United States. The Anasazi flourished from about 300 B.C. to A.D. 1300 in the

*An Indian priest wearing traditional jewelry worships a god from atop a temple mound. The Hopewell Indians of the eastern United States buried their dead in these huge mounds.*

area where the present-day states of Colorado, Utah, Arizona, and New Mexico meet.

During religious rituals and ceremonial dances, Anasazi Indians put on bright costumes and turquoise jewelry in the belief that the sparkling, deep-blue stone had powers that could protect the wearer from harm. Anasazi jewelers often combined turquoise with seashells or bones to make exquisite beads, pendants, and gorgets.

Native American jewelry techniques underwent great change after Europeans settled in North America. From the Europeans the Indians learned how to work metals, particularly silver. The Indians also traded with the Europeans for glass beads, which artisans used to decorate clothing, headbands, and pouches. These crafts continue to flourish in modern times, providing archaeologists with a link to North America's past.

## Making Modern Jewelry

Modern people wear jewelry for many of the same reasons that an-

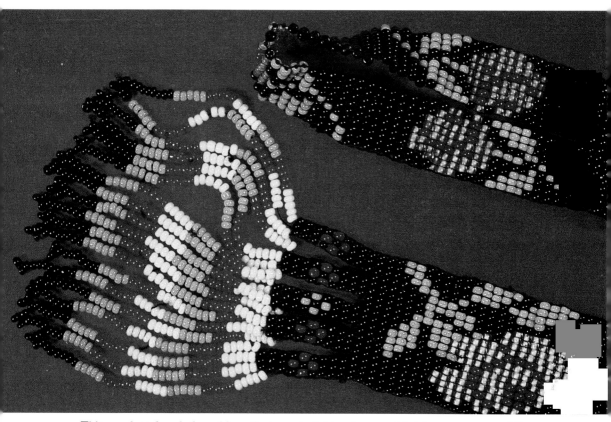

*This modern beaded necklace features bright colors and intricate patterns. Many present-day Native Americans carry on the traditional craft of beadwork.*

*Wearing protective glasses, a jeweler heats metal to form it into the desired shape. Although much fine jewelry is crafted by hand, a large amount of modern jewelry is made by machine.*

cient people did. Some pieces have important religious or superstitious significance. Elaborate or expensive gems serve to display the wealth and importance of an individual. Many people wear jewelry for sentimental reasons or simply for decoration.

Making jewelry by hand is still an important art form. Jewelers and artisans painstakingly cut gems and shape metals to create beautiful, expensive pieces. Many traditional craftspeople continue jewelry-making customs started by their ancestors. Some Native American artists, for example, produce intricate silver and turquoise jewelry or create pieces of elaborate beadwork. These artisans often sell their traditional wares at art shows and festivals, as well as in fine jewelry stores.

Most modern jewelry, however, is produced in mass quantities. Huge machines shape metal earrings, pendants, and pins. Clasps are attached systematically with solder or glue and molds turn out large numbers of identical pieces. This factory-made jewelry is usually sold in department stores, rather than in specialized jewelry shops.

Just as archaeologists have studied the jewelry-making techniques, materials, and styles of past civilizations, experts continue to examine how jewelry relates to modern life. As cultures change, so do their customs, and these changes are often reflected in how individuals adorn themselves.

# PRONUNCIATION GUIDE

agate (AG-eht)

ajouré (ah-zhoo-RAY)

Anasazi (ahn-uh-SAHZ-ee)

cloisonné (klawz-uhn-AY)

Euphrates (yoo-FRAYT-eez)

faience (fay-AHNTS)

fibula (FIHB-yuh-luh)

gorget (GOR-juht)

Huang (HWANG)

lapis lazuli (lap-uhs LA-zuh-lee)

Maya (MY-uh)

Mesopotamia
    (mehs-uh-puh-TAY-mee-uh)

Moche (MOH-chay)

Mycenae (my-SEE-nee)

*opus interrasile*
    (OH-puhs ihn-teh-rah-SEE-lay)

pharaoh (FEHR-oh)

Phoenician (fih-NEESH-uhn)

repoussé (ruh-poo-SAY)

torque (TAWRK)

Tutankhamen
    (too-tan-KAHM-uhn)

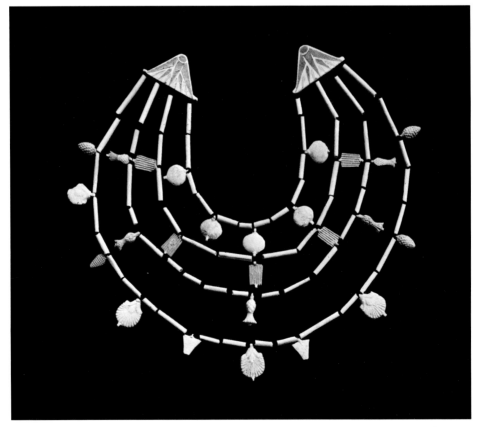

*Ancient jewelers crafted the dangling shapes of this delicate necklace from faience.*

# GLOSSARY

**This ancient gold earring consists of beads hanging from a fierce face.**

**afterlife:** an existence after death.

**ajouré:** any kind of openwork pattern.

**alloy:** a metal that is a mixture of two or more metals.

**archaeologist:** a scientist who studies the material remains of past human life.

**chasing:** a metalworking technique in which the artist hammers on the front of the piece so that the pattern is indented in the metal.

**cloisonné:** a style of enamel decoration in which a network of raised cells (cloisons) forms a pattern on a metal background. Colored enamels are poured into the cells and baked. When cooled and hardened, the enamel is polished.

**excavate:** to dig out and remove objects from an archaeological site.

**faience:** a glaze that imitates the color and shine of semiprecious stones.

**filigree:** delicate, lacy metalwork. Ancient jewelers often twisted gold or silver wire into filigree patterns.

**granulation:** the process of decorating jewelry by soldering tiny metal grains to the surface of the ornament.

**inlay:** to set a material, such as shell or stones, into a flat surface to form a decoration.

**labret:** an ornament for the lip.

**lapidary:** a person who cuts and polishes precious stones.

**niello:** a method of decorating the surface of a metal object with a black compound of sulfur that is applied in patterns. The object is then heated, melting the powdery compound onto the metal surface.

**opus interrasile:** a pierced metalworking method in which an artist cuts out a pattern from a sheet of gold using awls or tiny chisels.

**repoussé:** a technique of decoration in which a design is hammered into the back of a metal sheet, causing the pattern to be raised from the surface on the front side.

**setting:** the frame or mounting in which gemstones or other decorative items are held.

**solder:** to join by melting metals together.

# INDEX

*Excavators in Egypt recovered this colorful pectoral shaped like a falcon from Tutankhamen's tomb.*

*A gem cutter examines the shape and clarity of a diamond.*

## Photo Acknowledgments

Lynn Abercrombie, p. 2; Photographic Archive, Bruning Museum, p. 7, 55 (bottom); Independent Picture Service, pp. 9, 12 (bottom), 13 (top and bottom), 14, 18, 21, 24, 25, 35, 40 (bottom), 44, 60; Alex Kerstich, p. 10; Z. Rodovan, Jerusalem, p. 11; Gemco International/by Kathy Raskob/IPS, p. 15 (top); SATOUR, p. 15 (bottom); Steven J. Truax, by Kathy Raskob/IPS, pp. 16, 63; British Museum, pp. 8, 12 (top), 17, 18, 19, 22, 23, 29, 36, 39, 40 (bottom), 41, 42, 46, 51, 52; Griffith Institute, Ashmolean Museum, Oxford, p. 27; Nelson-Atkins Museum of Art, p. 30 (top and bottom); Berthold Laufer, *Jade: A Study in Chinese Archaeology and Religion* (South Pasadena, Calif.: P.D. and Ione Perkins, 1946), p. 31; The Metropolitan Museum of Art, Samuel Eilenberg Collection, Gift of Samuel Eilenberg, 1987. (1987.142.290), p. 32; Asian Art Museum of San Francisco, p. 33; National Museum of Ireland, p. 43; Ashmolean Museum, Oxford, pp. 45, 48; Staatliche Museen, Bildarchiv Preussischer Kulturbesitz, p. 47; The Mansell Collection, pp. 37, 49; Werner Forman Archive/British Museum, London, p. 54; Christopher Donnan, p. 55 (top); Tennessee State Museum, from a painting by Carlyle Urello, p. 57; Lucille Sukalo, p. 58; Paula Jansen, p. 59; Library of Congress, p. 61; University of Minnesota College of Architecture and Landscape Architecture, p. 62.

Cover photographs: Nelson-Atkins Museum of Art (front) and Paula Jansen (back).